Math Tutor Lesson Plan Series

Pre-Algebra: Grades 6-8 Math Tutor Lesson Plan Series

iGlobal ™
Educational Services
Believe.Inspire.Transform.

iGlobal Educational Services

Table of Contents

Introduction

Introduction

Tutoring is beginning to get the respect and recognition it deserves. More and more learners require in-dividualized or small group instruction whether it is in the classroom setting or in a private tutoring setting either face-to-face or online.

This lesson plan book is part of the "Math Tutor Lesson Plan" Series. It is conceived and created for tutors and educators who desire to provide effective tutoring either in person or online in any educational set-ting, including the classroom.

Inside This Lesson Plan Book

This *Pre-Algebra: Grades 6-8: Math Tutor Lesson Plan Series* book provides appropriate practice during tutoring sessions for learners for both face-to-face and online tutoring sessions focused on topics in Pre-Algebra: Grades 6-8.

The goal of the *Pre-Algebra: Grades 6-8: Math Tutor Lesson Plan Series* book is to support all types of tutors. Also, this book is to support teachers who want to provide in-class tutoring to their students in either an individualized or small group tutoring setting. Lastly, this book is also for teachers who are providing math intervention either individually or in small group tutoring sessions either face to face or online so that they can select the specific lesson plan to address the learner's math learning needs.

How to Use This Lesson Plan Book

iGlobal Educational Services, created this tutoring resource to help with designing effective tutoring in-struction for tutors and teachers who desire to provide in-class tutoring sessions.

These specific lessons were selected based upon field-tested experiences with learners who had learn-ing needs over the years in these specific areas in mathematics. We have provided learning objectives and specific topics covered in each tutoring session so that you can align them with your state's specific standards or adapted standards. For overseas tutors, you can follow suite and align the lesson objectives to specific educational standards required in your country.

These lesson plans should be used to supplement a strong and viable curriculum that encourages differ-entiation for all diverse learners. They can be used in individual or small group tutoring sessions conduct-ed face-to-face or online in any educational setting, including the classroom.

Organization of the Lesson Plan Book

Rather than provide a specific "curriculum" to follow, *Pre-Algebra: Grades 6-8: Math Tutor Lesson Plan Series* book provides a blueprint to design effective tutoring lessons that are aligned with the *"Dr. Holland-Johnson's Session Review Framework"*. Tutor evaluators and coaches are able to analyze tutoring sessions and coach tutors when utilizing the *"Dr. Holland-Johnson's Lesson Plan Blueprint for Tutors"*. In each lesson plan, learners have an opportunity to focus on real-world connections, vocabulary, and practice the math concepts learned in the tutoring sessions in the appropriate amounts to learn and retain the content knowledge. Tutors will have an opportunity to provide direct and guided instruction, while learners practice concepts on their own during independent instruction.

Each lesson plan comes with a mini-assessment pertaining to the math concepts learned in the specific tutoring session. Depending on the learner's academic needs, the tutor or teacher will deem when it is appropriate to administer the mini-assessment. For online tutoring sessions or as an online option to take the mini-assessment, tutors and teachers can upload these mini-assessments to be completed online in their choice of an online assessment tool.

Lesson 1
Squares, Square Roots and Pythagorean Theorem

Lesson Description:

This lesson is designed to help students understand conceptually what is going on when they are asked to work with squares, square roots, and the Pythagorean Theorem. Please be sure to utilize the questions to help spark student engagement and cover the vocabulary that is associated with this specific tutoring session. For your own knowledge, sample responses have been provided to guide you as well.

Learning Objective:

In today's session, the learner will represent squares and square roots using geometric models.

Introduction

We understand that $3 \times 2 = 6$, $2 \times 2 \times 2^3 \times 3 =$. The numbers 6 and 24 that are expressed as a product of others are called **composite numbers** while the numbers whose product give rise to 6 and 24 are called **factors.** When factors are prime numbers, we call them **prime factors.**

In our discussion, we will have more interest in factors that are prime, prime or considered Prime Factors.

Now consider the composite number 25 and its prime factors.

We can express 25 as a product of its prime factors, thus $5 \times 5 = 25$. Such numbers having some interesting properties make our today's discussion.

Question 1

How can you find prime factors of a number ? cite an example

Response

Given the number, you divide it by prime numbers (that divide it completely) from the smallest, 2, until it reduces to 1 or another prime number. For instance , let the number be 105.

Be gin by 2, since 2 cannot divide 105 completely, we skip it and try 3.

3 divides it 35 times. 3 cannot divide 35, we go to the next one, 5.

5 divides 35 , 7 times.

The number has reduced to 7, a prime number.

Thus its prime factors are 3, 5 and 7.

Note that $3 \times 5 \times 7 = 105$

The method described above is called **prime factorization method.**

Specific Vocabulary for Tutoring Sessions

Composite numbers

Are numbers that can be expressed as a product of others numbers other than 1. Example, 20, 12, 345.

Factors

They are numbers that can divide others completely without a remainder. Example, 3, 5 and 9 are factors of 45.

Prime numbers

Are numbers whose factors are 1 and themselves. Example 2, 3, 11, 29.

Divisor

A number that divides another.

Dividend

A number that is divided by another.

Quotient

Is the result of division operation.

Prime factor

Are divisors of numbers that are prime numbers.

Squares

Is a product of two equal numbers. Example, the square of 4 is 16.

Square roots

Square root of a number is a number whose square gives the former. Example, the square root of 16 is 4.

Squares

A square is a product of a number by itself. For instance. $5 \times 5 = 25$. Thus the square of 5 is 25.

We denote the square of a number by a superscript 2.

Therefore , the square of 6 is $6^2 = 6 \times 6 = 36$.

If x is any number then its square is read as, **"x squared".**

Question 2

Find the square of

Response

We first simply 3 squared $3^2 = 3 \times 3 = 9$

We now find the square of 9.

The square of 9 is $9^2 = 9 \times 9 = 81$

Therefore, the square of   is 81.

Question 3

Millicent plans to tile the floor of her office. If the office is a square of side 10 feet, what is the area to be tiled?

Response

Area to be tiled is equal to the area of the square.

$\text{Area} = (side)^2 = 10^2 = 10 \times 10 = 100$ **square feet** .

Square roots

The square root of a number, says x, is a number whose square is x. For instance, the square root of 81 is 9 because $9^2 = 9 \times 9 = 81$. A square root is represented by a symbol " $\sqrt{}$ " called the square root symbol.

Therefore, the square root of 81 is $2+\frac{1}{3}\left(\frac{2^2}{10}+\frac{3}{4}\left(\frac{2}{2\times15}\right)\right)$

From the discussion of the product of integers, we found that the product negative numbers is a positive. Therefore, we may as well say that $2+\frac{1}{3}\left(\frac{2^2}{10}+\frac{3}{4}\left(\frac{2}{2\times15}\right)\right)$ since $-9 \times -9 = 9 \times 9 = 81$

Therefore, the square root of a number gives two numbers, a positive and a negative number.

In our discussion about square root, we will limit ourselves to the square roots of positive numbers only.

Illustrations on how to find the square root of a number.

Find the square root of   a). 144 b). 1225

We express 144 as a product of its prime factors using prime factorization method. This is best done in a table where the number is continuously divided by the prime factors.

144	72	36	18	9	3
2	2	2	2	3	

$144 = 2 \times 2 \times 2 \times 2 \times 3 \times 3 =$; $\sqrt{144} = \sqrt{2^4 \times 3^2}$

To find the square root of the product, we divide the subscripts (the powers) by 2.

Therefore

$\sqrt{1225}$

We express 1225 as a product of its prime factors using prime factorization method using the table below

1225	245	49	7
5	5	7	

$1225 = 5 \times 5 \times 7 \times 7 = 5^2 \times 7^2$; $\sqrt{1225} = \sqrt{5^2 \times 7^2}$

To find the square root of the product, we divide the subscripts (the powers) by 2. Therefore

$\sqrt{1225} = \sqrt{5^2 \times 7^2} = 5 \times 7 = 35$

To determine the square root of a number using the above method, the prime factors must have powers that are even, that can be divided by 2 completely.

Notice that the problems so far solved are integer square roots. The numbers whose square roots are positive integers are called **perfect squares.**

The above method is only used to find the square root of perfect squares only. What about the square root of other numbers like 12?. Remember $12 = 2^2 \times 3$, in this case we cannot determine the square root of 12 since 3 does not have a power that is even.

The method that can determine the square root of such number is called **the long division method.**

Question 4

James has a piece of land in form of a square of area 7056 square yards. If he wishes to plant trees along its perimeter, what distance should he consider when calculating the number of trees required to fence the whole piece of land?

Response

The distance to be considered is the distance all round the piece of land = perimeter

We first find the length of the side

Area = s^2 where s is the side.

Thus $7056 = s^2$

To find s, we determine the square root of both sides

$\sqrt{7056} = \sqrt{s^2} = s$

We express 7056 as a product of its prime factors using prime factorization

7056	3528	1764	882	441	147	49	7
2	2	2	2	3	3	7	

Thus $7056 = 2 \times 2 \times 2 \times 2 \times 3 \times 3 \times 7 \times 7 = \sqrt{7056} = \sqrt{2^4 \times 3^2 \times 7^2}$

To find the square root of the product, we divide the subscripts (the powers) by 2. Therefore

$\sqrt{7056} = \sqrt{2^4 \times 3^2 \times 7^2} = 2^2 \times 3 \times 7 = 2 \times 2 \times 3 \times 7 = 84$ or -84

Since the side is a measurement which must be positive, we ignore the negative answer.

Side = 84 yards

Perimeter = 84 + 84 + 84 + 84 = 336 square yards

Square root by long division
We will describe this by an example

Find the square root of 131044

First, we group the digits in pairs beginning from the right as shown 13 10 44

We then consider the first pair, 13

We find a number whose square is equal to or closer but less 13. The number is 3 since its square, 9, is closer and less than 13.

We then write 3 at the position of the divisor and the quotient

$$\begin{array}{ccccc} & & 3 & & \\ 3 & 13 & 10 & 44 \end{array}$$

We then multiply 3 by 3 (divisor by quotient) to get 9 and subtract 9 from 13 . We also add 3 (the divisor) to 3 (the quotient) to get 6 and write it below 3, the divisor as shown below. We then put two bracket as shown below and bring down 10 to have 410.

```
        3              ()
        3     13    10      44
             - 9
     6 ()      4    10
```

We then look for a number such that when we put in the two brackets, its product and that of the number beginning with 6 will be equal to or less than but closest to 4 10. For instance, if the number is 1, then we will have 1 in the bracket above 10 and 1 next to 6 so that the product of 1 and 61 would be less but closest to 410. The suitable number is 6. Thus, we have 66 and a 6 in the bracket above 10. The product of 6 and 66 will be 396. We then subtract 396 from 410 and bring down 44.

Again, we add 66 (the divisor) to 6 (quotient) and write the answer (72) below it with a bracket next to it. We also write a bracket above 44

```
         3    (6)
     3   13   10   44
         - 9
   66     4  10
         -3  96
 72()        14  44
```

We then look for a number such that when we put in the two brackets, its product and that of the number beginning with 72 will be equal to or less than but closest to 14 44. The best number is 2.

```
         3    (6)  (2)
     3   13  10    44
         - 9
   66     4  10
         -3  96
 72(2)       14  44
            -14  44
                  0
```

Therefore, the square root of 131044 is 362 or -362

This method can also be used to find the square root of a number that is not a perfect square.

Question 5

Find the square root of 23445. Write your answer to the nearest whole number.

Response

We group the number in pairs beginning from the right; 2 34 45

The square of a number equal to or less than but closer to 2 will be 1. Thus

```
          1
   1    2   34 45
       -1
        1
```

We add 1 (the divisor) to 1 (the quotient) then write the answer , 2, with a bracket below 1 the divisor. We also put a bracket above 34. We the bring 34 down to have 134. The best number will be 5.

```
        1    (5)
   1    2   34 45
       -1
  2(5)  1  34
```

We multiply 25 by 5 then subtract the answer from 134 to get 9. We the bring down 45.

```
        1    (5)
   1    2   34 45
       -1
  2(5)  1  34
      - 1  25
          9  45
```

We add 5 to 25 to get 30 . We write 30, with a bracket after it, below 25. The suitable number for the bracket is 9

```
         1   (5)  ()
   1    2   34 45
        -1
   2(5)  1  34
       -1  25
 30()        9  45
         1   (5)  (3)
   1    2   34  45
        -1
   2(5)  1  34
       -1  25
 30(3)       9  45
           -9  09
               36
```

We proceed so that we get at least one decimal place so that we can round off to the nearest whole number. Since we have exhausted all the numbers, we bring down 2 zeros then put a decimal place after 3 in the quotient.

We then add 303 to 3 to get 306 put a bracket next to it below 303. We also put a bracket next to the decimal place.

```
            1    (5)  (3) . (1)
        1    2    34   45
            -1
      2(5)  1   34
            -1   25
      30(3)      9   45
               -9   09
    306 (1)        36  00
```

Therefore the square root of 23445 is 153.1

Since we must have the answer to the nearest whole number which begins from 3 to the left, we look the next number to the right, 1, since it is less than 5, we ignore it and add zero to 3. The final result is 153.

Therefore $\sqrt{23445}$ ≈ +153 or − 153

Question 6

Pamuy has a square garden whose area is 163 square feet. What would be the length of one side?

Response

The area = s^2 = 163

Thus side = s = $\sqrt{163}$

To find the square root of 163, we use the long division method since it not a perfect square.

We divide the number into pairs from the right, that is 1 63

Considering the first number, we get the number whose square is 1, the number is 1, thus we have the following:

```
            1
      1   1  63
          -1
          0   63
```

We then add 1(divisor) to 1 (quotient) the right the result, 2, below 1 the divisor and put a bracket next to it. We also put a bracket above 59.

```
        1   ()
    1   1  63
        -1
   2()   0  63
```

The best number that when put in the bracket so that the product of the number and the number beginning with 2 be equal to or less but closest to 63 is 2.

The product of 2 and 22 will be 44 so that the difference between 63 and 22 can be determined.

```
        1   (2)
    1   1  63
        -1
   2(2) 0   63
          - 44
            19
```

We bring down 2 zeros to have 1900 and put a decimal after 2 in the quotient. We add 22 to 2 then write the answer in below 22 and put the bracket next to it. The best number that can fill bracket is 7.

```
               1   (2) . (7)
           1   1   63
               -1
       2(2)    0   63
                 - 44
   24(7)        19 00
                - 17 29
                  171
```

Therefore, the square root of 163 is approximately 12.7 feet.

Therefore, the side of Pamuy 's garden measures 12.7 feet.

Pythagorean Theorem

Pythagorean Theorem is a relation that relates the sides of a triangle, however the triangle must satisfy some conditions.

In our study about triangle, we learnt that there are four types of triangle; the scalene triangle, the Isosceles triangle, the equilateral triangle and the right angle triangle. Our focus is on a right angle triangle.

A right angle triangle is a triangle where one of its angle measures 90°. This angle is at the intersection of two sides of a triangle usually referred to as the base and the height. The angle opposite to the longest side of the triangle called the hypotenuse.

Let the length of the base be *b*, that of the height be *a* and that of the hypotenuse be *c*, then we have the following diagram.

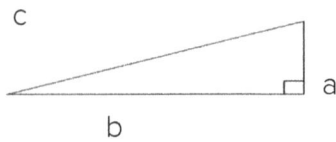

Whenever *a* and *b* are perpendicular (intersect each other at 90°) , are shorter sides of a right angle triangle, then a, b and c are given by

This means that the sum of the square of the smaller sides of a right angle triangle is equal to the square of the larger side.

From the relation   we have $c = \sqrt{a^2 + b^2}$

$$a = \sqrt{c^2 - b^2}$$

$$b = \sqrt{c^2 - a^2}$$

Question 7

Find the base of a right angle triangle whose hypotenuse is 25 inches and the height 7 inches.

Response

Let the base be b, the hypotenuse be c = 25 inches and the height be a = 7 inches.

Using Pythagorean theorem $c^2 = a^2 + b^2$

The base b is given by $b = \sqrt{c^2 - a^2}$

Upon substitution, we have $b = \sqrt{25^2 - 7^2} = \sqrt{625 - 49}$

$$= \sqrt{576} = 24 \ \text{inches}$$

Therefore, the base measures 24 inches

Question 8

Amos has a rectangular piece of land that measures 120 yards by 50 yards. If the land is to be divided into two equal parts along the diagonal. What would be the length of the diagonal.

Response

The diagonal divides the piece of land into two equal right triangles where the shorter sides measures 129 yards and 50 yards respectively and the longer side is the hypotenuse.

Using Pythagorean theorem; $a^2 + b^2 = c^2$ and $c = \sqrt{a^2 + b^2}$ where the letters have their usual meaning.

Upon substitution, we have

$$c = \sqrt{a^2 + b^2} = \sqrt{120^2 + 50^2} = \sqrt{14400 + 2500} = \sqrt{16900} = 130 inches$$

The diagonal measures 130 inches

Video Suggestions for Tutoring Sessions

Please conduct a search on either YouTube or TeacherTube to find appropriate videos for this lesson. Below are some suggested title searches:

Pythagorean Theorem in Architectural Constructions

Pythagorean Theorem in Football and Games

Pythagorean Theorem in Shooting a Ball

Independent Instruction: Working on your Own

Questions

1. Evaluate the $\sqrt{81}$ then find its square.

2. Find the square root of 676

3. Determine the square root of $\sqrt{48}$ to the nearest one decimal place.

Responses

1. We first find the square root of 81.

   We express 81 as a product of its prime factors. Using prime factorization, we have

81	27	9	3
3	3	3	

   $81 = 3 \times 3 \times 3 \times 3 = $; $\sqrt{81} = \sqrt{3^4} = 3^2$ (upon dividing the superscript by 2) The square root of 81 is $3 \times 3 = 9$

   The square of 9 is $9^2 = 9 \times 9 = 81$

2. To find the square root we first express 576 as a product of its prime factors. Using prime factorization we have

676	338	169	13
2	2	13	

   $676 = 2 \times 2 \times 13 \times 13$

   $676 = 2^2 \times 13^2$

   $\sqrt{676} = \sqrt{2^2 \times 13^2}$

   $\sqrt{2^2 \times 13^2} = 2 \times 13 = 26$

3. Since the number has two digit , we proceed with the process

   ```
         6
     6 ⌐48
       -36
        12
   ```

   We add 6 the divisor to 6 the quotient and write the result 12 and a bracket next to it below 6, the quotient. Since we must have the answer written to 1 decimal places, we must have the quotient having 2 decimal places. We bring down two zeros then put a decimal after 6 (the quotient). We the put a bracket after the decimal.

```
              6 . ()
       6    48
           -36
      12()    1200
```

The best number that fills the bracket is

```
              6 . (9)
       6    48
           -36
     12(9)   1200
            -1161
              39 00
```

We multiply 9 by 129 and subtract the results from 1200. We then add 9 to 129 (to get 1388) the right the answer, with a bracket beside it. We also bring down two zeros to make 3900.

```
              6 . (9) (2)
       6    48
           -36
     12(9)  1200
           -1161
    138(2)    39 00
```

The square root is 6.92. To have one decimal place number, we find out if the number to the right of 9 is more than 5. Since it is less than 5, we ignore it and add zero to 9 to get 6.9

Therefore, the square root of 48 is approximately 6.9.

Mini assessment

1 12 inches square tiles are to be used to tile a rectangular floor measuring 108 inches by 132 inches. How many such tiles are required.

   A. 99   B. 72   C. 144   D. 40   E. 1188

2 A student takes 2 minutes to run from one corner to an opposite corner of a soccer field. If the field measures 80 yards by 60 yards determine her speed in yards per minute.

   A. 10 yards/min   B. 26 yards/min   C. 12 yards/min
   D. 5 yards/min   E. 25 yards/min

3 Find the area of a square of side 49 inches.

   A. 7 square inches   B. 28 square inches   C. 2401 square inches
   D. 98 square inches   E. 196 square inches

4 Find the number of poles required to fence a square piece of land of 1764 square yard spaced at a distance of 3 feet from each other.

5 A 61 inches larder is placed against a wall. If the larder grips the wall at a 60 inches height point, how far is the larder from the foot of the wall?

6 A pilot flying at a height of 15 yards above a national park notices an polar bear on the ground 17 yards from her location. How far is the bear from a point that is vertically below the plane?

7 Mercy wishes to make a square based water tank of base area 9 square feet and a height of 4 feet. If the tank is to be filled with water for construction purposes, calculate the surface of the tank in contact with water.

Mini-Assessment Answers

1 A
The area of the tile is 12 × 12 = 144
The area of the floor = 108 × 132 = 14,256
The number of tiles required = $\dfrac{14256}{144} = 99$

2 D
A soccer field is in the form of a rectangle of 80 yards by 60yards
The distance from one corner to the opposite is the a diagonal, hypotenuse of a triangle whose shorter sides measure 80 yards by 60yards.

By Pythagorean theorem, the $c^2 = 8^2 + 6^2$; $c = \sqrt{8^2 + 6^2} = \sqrt{100} = 10\,yards$

Speed = $\dfrac{Dis\tan ce}{time} = \dfrac{10}{2} = 5\,yards\,/\,Minute$

3 C
Area = side × side = 49 × 49 = 2401 square inches

4 Area = s^2 = 1764 square yards
s = √1764
Using prime factorization
1764 = 2 × 2 × 3 × 3 × 7 × 7 = $2^2 \times 3^2 \times 7^2$
$\sqrt{1764} = \sqrt{2^2 \times 3^2 \times 7^2} = 2 \times 3 \times 7 = 42$
Side = 42 yards
One yard = 3 feet, thus the distance between one pole from another will be 1 yard.
All round the piece of land, we will have 42 × 4 =168 − 1 = 167 poles

5 The hypotenuse is the larder = 61 inches
$b = \sqrt{61^2 - 60^2} = \sqrt{3721 - 3600} = \sqrt{121} = \sqrt{11^2} = 11\,inches$ The height = 60 inches
Base is given by Pythagorean theorem,

6 The hypotenuse is the distance from the pilot to the bear = 17 yards
Height = 15
Base = distance from the bear to the point below the plane is give by Pythagorean theorem
$b = \sqrt{17^2 - 15^2} = \sqrt{289 - 225} = \sqrt{64} = \sqrt{2^6} = 2^3 = 8\,yards$ the required distance is 8 yards

7 The area of the base = 9 square feet
The length of the side is the square root of 9 = 3 feet
When filled with water the vertical and the bottom faces will get into contact with water.
Thus, the total surface area will be in contact with water is
(3 × 3) + 4(3 × 4) = 9 + 4(12) = 57 square feet

Lesson Reflection

- In this lesson, we have learned about squares and square roots. A square of a number is the product of the number by itself while the square root of a number , say t, is a number whose square is t. We went ahead and discussed two major methods of finding square roots, the prime factorization method and the long division method.

- The discussion of the square and the square roots leads to Pythagorean theorem which is widely applied in day to day life.

Lesson 2
Irrational Numbers: Scientific Notation and Exponent Rules

Lesson Description:

This lesson is designed to help students understand conceptually what is going on when they are asked to work with irrational numbers, specifically scientific notation and exponents. Please be sure to utilize the questions to help spark student engagement and cover the vocabulary that is associated with this specific tutoring session. For your own knowledge, sample responses have been provided to guide you as well.

Learning Objective:

In today's session, the learner will convert between standard decimal notation and scientific notation.

Introduction

In most cases, we have dealt with numbers such as 21, 0, -2, 4, $\frac{4}{15}$, 0.002, among others.

The most common thing about these numbers is that they can be written in the form $\frac{h}{k}$ where the two numbers, h and k are integers that do not have a common factor k is not zero. Such numbers are called **Rational number.** Therefore, in most of our day to day life and calculations, we deal with rational numbers. However, there is yet another group of numbers that we interact with in our day to day life without knowing dues to their unique appearance. We do not usually realize them because they represent sophisticated natural activities and occurrences that one may simply explain (not to the fullest) but not understand what they are and why they happen. Such activities include decay among others. These numbers are called **irrational numbers.**

Rounding off

This is a concept that is usually used to estimate numbers by reducing or increasing their values while reducing the number of digits the number originally had. We will assume that we are all familiar with the concept of place value and decimal numbers. For instance, when a number such as 45.871 is to be written to two decimal places, then it should have 2 digits after the decimal place. The second digit is 7; we now check if the number in the third decimal place is more or less than 5. If more or less than 5, we add 1 or zero respectively to the second digit then ignore all the other digits that comes after the second digit. Therefore 45.871 will be 45.87 or 45.9 to two decimal places or one decimal place respectively.

This concept of rounding off is used to approximate irrational numbers.

Question 1
Why do you think rounding off is also important to some rational number too?

Response
When working with long rational numbers such as 234. 70052013, it may be important to round it off so that it can have few digits that one can easily handle to avoid simple mistakes and time wastage. In some situations, some figures after the second, third or so, decimal places may not be that significant to be retained. For instance, most currencies work with numbers that have at most 2 decimal places.

Specific Vocabulary for Tutoring Session

Rational number
Is a number that can be expressed as h/k where h and k are integers and k cannot be zero. Examples ½, 3, 0.6, -5,..

Irrational numbers
It is a number that cannot be expressed as h/k where h and k are integers and k cannot be zero. Examples pi =π

Rounding off
It is a way of approximating a number by reducing the number of its digits under some conditions. Example, 24 is rounded off to the nearest tens to 20.

Euler's number
It an irrational number that is given as $e = 2.7182818...$

Exponential notation
It is a way of representing a number say 9 in the form 3^2 where 3 is called the **base** and 2 **the exponent, power or index.**

Scientific notation

A number is written in scientific notation if it is written in the form where *a* is a number that is less than 10 but equal to or more than 1 and n is an integer.

Irrational numbers

Irrational numbers are numbers that cannot take a form of a rational number therefore, they cannot be written in their exact value as fractions. They are expressed as non terminating decimals thus, they are simply approximated. Some of this numbers are *e, pi = π* among others.

For example, 45.08413.... is an irrational number since when numbers after the decimal does not appear in pattern , and when listed, they are do not end. In our usual calculations, we represent irrational numbers with their estimates or sometimes round them off to a certain number of desired decimal places then use them. Apart from representing them as decimals, some irrational number are represented as roots.

The most common irrational numbers are; roots example √2 , *e* called **Euler's number**, *π* called pi,ϕ called the **golden ratio** among others.

> The following list shows irrational numbers rounded off to 7 decimal places

$\sqrt{2} = 1.4142136$

$e = 2.7182818$

$\pi = 3.1415927$

$\phi = 1.6180340$

Some of these numbers can be expressed in others forms or manipulated by other algebraic operations to give different numbers. For instance

1. $\pi = C \div d$ where C is a circumference of an ideal circle and d its radius. There are many approximations of pi however, the most commonly used is $\frac{22}{7}$

2. $\phi = \frac{1+\sqrt{5}}{2}$

Some operations on irrational numbers.
1. The sum or difference of two irrational numbers is irrational number
2. The product or the division of an irrational numbers/rational number and by a rational number/irrational number is always a rational number.
    Example $0.2 \div \phi$ or $\phi \div 0.2$ is an irrational number
    $54 \times \sqrt{7} = 54\sqrt{7}$ which is a irrational number

Question 2

Using an example, explain why the square of an irrational number is not always irrational.

Response

We consider irrationals numbers that have roots example $\sqrt{7}$

$$(\sqrt{7})^2 = \sqrt{7} \times \sqrt{7} = \sqrt{7 \times 7} = \sqrt{49} = 7$$

Since $7 = \dfrac{7}{1}$, it is a rational number

Question 3

Identify a rational number from the following list.

A. π^2

B. $\left(\sqrt{2}-1\right)\left(\sqrt{2}+1\right)$

C. ϕ^2

D. $3(2e+4e)$

E. $\dfrac{\phi+2}{0.003}$

Response

we study the numbers one by one to see if the are rational or irrational.

$\pi^2 = \pi \times \pi = 3.1415927... \times 3.1415927.....$

This number cannot have a fraction representation, therefore, it is irrational.

We therefore more to the next number

$$\left(\sqrt{2}-1\right)\left(\sqrt{2}+1\right) = \sqrt{2}\left(\sqrt{2}+1\right) - 1\left(\sqrt{2}+1\right)$$

$$= \sqrt{2}\sqrt{2} + 1\sqrt{2} - 1\sqrt{2} - 1$$

$$= \sqrt{2 \times 2} + \sqrt{2} - \sqrt{2} - 1$$

$$= 2 + \sqrt{2} - \sqrt{2} - 1$$

$$= 2 - 1 = 1$$

The result is 1 a rational number. We do not need to test the other numbers because we already have the answer.

Therefore, the answer is B

Scientific notation

We will revisit the representation of squares. Remember that $9 = 3 \times 3 = 3^2$

Thus 3^2 means 3 is multiplied 2 times by itself.

Using the same argument, we say that ___ means that 3 is multiplied 7 times by itself

$$10^5 \text{ means that 10 is multiplied 5 times by itself}$$

A number is written in scientific notation if it is written in the form $a + 10^n$

where a is a number that is less than 10 but equal to or more than 1 and n is an integer. This implies that a can be a positive whole number or a decimal number less than 10.

n is a integer, therefore, it can be positive or negative

A number written in scientific notation is said to be in **standard form.**

Let us consider the following numbers.

(a) 6921

To have an a less than 10, we must have a decimal point between 6 and 9

Thus a = 6.921

Since 6921 = 6.921 × 1000, we have $6921 = 6.921 \times 10^3$

Something important worthy noting here is the movement of the decimal point. A decimal point is always after the number in the once position. In this case, the decimal in 6921 is after 1. After writing the number in scientific notation, it moves three steps to the right to 6.921.

Therefore, in writing the scientific notation of a number, the power of 10 (value of n) is equal to the number of steps moved by the decimal point and is positive when the decimal moves to the left.

(b) 853. 561

To have the number , a, being less than 10, we place the decimal point between 8 and 5. The decimal point would have moved 2 steps to the left, thus n = 2.

$853. 561 = 8.53561 \times 10^2$

(c) 0.0471

To have the number, a, being more or equal to 1 and less than 10, we place the decimal point between 4 and 7. The decimal point will have moved 2 steps to the right. In this case, the point moves in the opposite direction as compared to example (a) and (b), thus n = -2.

$$0.0471 = 4.71 \times 10^{-2} \text{ note that } 10^{-2} = \frac{1}{10^2} = \frac{1}{100}$$

(d) 0.000001

In this case, we place the decimal point after 1 . The former would have moved 6 steps to the right, thus n = -6.

$$0.000001 = 1.0 \times 10^{-6} \text{ note that } 10^{-6} = \frac{1}{10^6} = \frac{1}{1,000,000}$$

Negative numbers can also be written in scientific notation where a will be negative while n will depend on the value of the number.

Questions 4

USA is estimated to have an area of 3794100 square miles. Express the area in standard form.

Response

First, we find the value of a.

We place the decimal place between 3 and 7 so that a = 3.7941

Since the decimal was after the last zero, it would have moved 6 steps to the left, hence n = 6

Therefore, the area is 3.7941×10^6 **square miles**

Question 5

The mass of an proton is 0.0000 0000 0000 0000 0000 0000 003688 pounds. Express the mass in scientific form.

Response

We find the value of a

Since a should be between 1 and 10 or 1, the only possible value is a = 3.688

By placing the decimal place between 2 and 6, we would have moved it 27 steps to the right, hence n = -27.

Therefore the mass of a proton is 3.688×10^{-27} **pounds**

Exponents and exponent rules

We have already seen that a number say 16 can be written in the form $16 = 2^4$ where 2 is referred to as a base and 4 an exponent, power or an index. A number written in terms of a base and an index is said to be in its **exponent form or exponential notation.**

We would like now to investigate and come up with rules on how to multiply and divide numbers in exponent form.

Multiplication rule

Remember that 100 × 1000 = 100,0000

But $100 = 10^2$, $1000 = 10^3$ and $100,000 = 10^5$

Therefore it is true to say that $10^2 \times 10^3 = 10^{2+3} = 10^5$

This is **the product rule of the exponent**, that whenever two number are given in an index form with the same base, then their product is arrived at by adding their exponent.

$$t^a \times t^b = t^{a+b}$$

Division rule

We will still use a similar example.

$100,0000 \div 100 = 1000$

Substituting the numbers using their exponential representatives, we have $10^5 \div 10^2 = 10^{5-2} = 10^3$

Thus the division of numbers with the same base implies the subtraction of their exponents.

$$t^a \div t^b = \frac{t^a}{t^b} = t^{a-b}$$

Double index rule

Consider the square to 1000

$1000^2 = 1000 \times 1000 = 1000,000 =$ in index notation

But $1000^2 = \left(10^3\right)^2$

Therefore, we have $1000^2 = \left(10^3\right)^2$ and

Then we must have $\left(10^3\right)^2 = 10^{3 \times 2} = 10^6$

$$\left(t^a\right)^b = t^{ab}$$

Definition of 1 in exponent form

It is obvious that b $100 \div 100 = 1$, but $100 \div 100 = 10^2 \div 10^2 = 10^{2-2} = 10^0$

Therefore $10^0 = 1$

Using any base, we get the same results, therefore, 1 is defined as any number raised to power zero.

Another rules

(1) $\frac{n^x}{m^x} = \left(\frac{n}{m}\right)^x$

Example, $\frac{2^3}{8^3} = \left(\frac{2}{8}\right)^3 = \left(\frac{1}{4}\right)^3 = \frac{1^3}{4^3} = \frac{1}{64}$

(2) 1 raised to the power of any number is just equal to 1

Addition and subtraction of numbers in index form

There is no exponent rule on adding or subtracting numbers in exponent form ,therefore when given such a problem, we first change the numbers to their standard value and add or subtract.

Example $3^5 - 3^2 = 243 - 9 = 234$

$\qquad 3^4 - 2^4 = 81 - 16 = 65$

Question 6

Use exponential notation to simplify the following problem

$$\frac{8\times32}{81}\div\frac{16}{72}$$

Response

$$\frac{8\times32}{81}\div\frac{16}{72}$$

We first change the numbers into their exponential notation $\dfrac{8\times32}{81}\div\dfrac{16}{72}=\dfrac{2^3\times2^5}{3^4}\div\dfrac{2^4}{2^3\times3^2}$

Note that 72 = 8 × 9

Using the definition of a division as a multiplication by reciprocal, we have $\dfrac{2^3\times2^5}{3^4}\times\dfrac{2^3\times3^2}{2^4}=\dfrac{2^3\times2^5\times2^3\times3^2}{3^4\times2^4}$

We now apply the multiplication law of exponents to powers with the same base

$$\frac{2^3\times2^5\times2^3\times3^2}{3^4\times2^4}=\frac{2^{3+5+3}\times3^2}{3^4\times2^4}=\frac{2^{11}\times3^2}{3^4\times2^4}$$

We now apply the division law of exponents to powers with the same base

$$\frac{2^{11}\times3^2}{3^4\times2^4}=\frac{2^{11}\times3^2}{2^4\times3^4}=2^{11-4}\times3^{2-4}=2^7\times3^{-2}$$

We simplify further using the division rule $2^7\times3^{-2}=2^7\times3^{0-2}=2^7\times\dfrac{3^0}{3^2}$

Using the definition of 1, we have $2^7\times\dfrac{3^0}{3^2}=2^7\times\dfrac{1}{3^2}=\dfrac{2^7}{3^2}$

Upon simplification, we have $\dfrac{2^7}{3^2}=\dfrac{128}{9}=14\dfrac{2}{9}$

Question 7

Simplify the following $\dfrac{a^2bc\times cd^2}{c^4d^{-3}a}$

Response

In this case, the bases are alphabetical numbers. The rule of exponents still applies.

$$\frac{a^2bc\times cd^2}{c^4d^{-3}a}=\frac{a^2bc^1\times c^1d^2}{c^4d^{-3}a}=\frac{a^2bc^{1+1}d^2}{c^4d^{-3}a}=\frac{a^2bc^2d^2}{c^4d^{-3}a}$$

We begin by applying the multiplication rule $\dfrac{a^2bc^2d^2}{c^4d^{-3}a}=\dfrac{a^2bc^2d^2}{ac^4d^{-3}}=\dfrac{a^2bc^2d^2}{a^1c^4d^{-3}}=a^{2-1}bc^{2-4}d^{2-(-3)}$

We the rearrange and apply the division rule $a^{2-1}bc^{2-4}d^{2-(-3)}=a^1bc^{-2}d^{2+3}=abc^{0-2}d^5$

Using the law of division, we have $abc^{0-2}d^5 = ab\dfrac{c^0}{c^2}d^5$

Using the definition of 1, we have $ab\dfrac{c^0}{c^2}d^5 = ab\dfrac{1}{c^2}d^5 = \dfrac{abd^5}{c^2}$

Question 8

The population of Missouri city is 2.1×10^3 million while that of Houston is thousand. How many times is Houston's population more than that of Missouri city?

Response

Houston's population = 2.1×10^3 thousand

Missouri city's population = 7.0×10^{-2} million

We change Missouri city's population to thousands so that the two values may be in thousands

1 million = 1000 thousand = 10^3 thousand

7.0×10^{-2} million = $7.0\times10^{-2}\times10^3 = 7.0\times10^{-2+3} = 7.0\times10$ thousands

Hoston's population will be $\dfrac{2.1\times10^3}{7.0\times10}$ times that of Missouri city $\dfrac{2.1\times10^3}{7.0\times10} = \dfrac{2.1}{7}\times10^{3-1}$ $\dfrac{2.1}{7}\times10^2 = 0.3\times10^2 = 30$

Hoston's population is 30 times that of Missouri's city

Question 9

In a survey to determine the number of Sitka Black-Tailed Deer in a section of Tongass National forest in Alaska, the investigating team began by covering acres. If they later extended their survey to 1.4 × 10 times the initial coverage, calculate the total area that was surveyed in million acres (write your answer is scientific notation).

Response

The initial coverage 4.2×10^5 acres

The increase was 1.4 × 10 times

The total coverage was the product; $4.2\times10^5\times1.4\times10 = 4.2\times1.4\times10^{5+1}$ acres

we use the multiplication law of exponents to carry multiplication

$= 4.2\times1.4\times10^6$ acres

On simplifying farther, we have

$= 5.88\times10^6$ acres

$= 5.88$ million acres

Video Suggestions for Tutoring Sessions

Please conduct a search on either YouTube or TeacherTube to find appropriate videos for this lesson. Below are some suggested title searches:

Scientific Notation in Writing Small and Large Numbers

Exponents and Distance

Distance in Terms of Exponents

Independent Instruction: Working on your Own

Questions

1. Identify an irrational number in the following list
   A. $2\sqrt{9}$
   B. $\dfrac{(\sqrt{2}-\sqrt{5})(\sqrt{2}+\sqrt{5})}{9}$
   C. $\dfrac{(1-\sqrt{5})(1+\sqrt{5})}{\sqrt{36}}$
   D. The square of $\sqrt{7}$
   E. $\left(\sqrt{2}\right)^{3}$

2. Convert the following number in its standard representation.
   0.000101×10^{5}

3. Edith plans to build a rectangular based complex whose area is 5.352048×10^{4} square feet. If its length is 3.812×10^{2} feet, determine its width.

Response

1. We simplify each number then decide the one that is irrational
   $2\sqrt{9} = 2 \times 3 = 6$ this is rational
   $$\dfrac{(\sqrt{2}-\sqrt{5})(\sqrt{2}+\sqrt{5})}{9} = \dfrac{\sqrt{2}(\sqrt{2}+\sqrt{5})-\sqrt{5}(\sqrt{2}+\sqrt{5})}{9}$$

$$= \frac{\sqrt{2}\sqrt{2} + \sqrt{5}\sqrt{2} - \sqrt{5}\sqrt{2} + \sqrt{5}\sqrt{5}}{9}$$ the number is rational

$$= \frac{2 + \sqrt{5}\sqrt{2} - \sqrt{5}\sqrt{2} + 5}{9} = \frac{7}{9}$$ the number is rational

$$\frac{(1-\sqrt{5})(1+\sqrt{5})}{\sqrt{36}} = \frac{1(1+\sqrt{5}) - \sqrt{5}(1+\sqrt{5})}{6}$$

$$= \frac{1 + \sqrt{5} - \sqrt{5} + 25}{6} = \frac{26}{6}$$ the number is rational

The square of $\sqrt{7}$ $\sqrt{7} \times \sqrt{7} = \sqrt{7 \times 7} = \sqrt{7^2} = 7$ is rational;

$$\left(\sqrt{2}\right)^3 = \sqrt{2} \times \sqrt{2} \times \sqrt{2} = \sqrt{2 \times 2} \times \sqrt{2} = 2 \times \sqrt{2} = 2\sqrt{2}$$ an irrational number.

The answer is E.

2. The number is in scientific notation where n = 5 . This implies that the decimal point was moved 5 times to the left. To get the number in its usual form, we move the decimal point 5 times to the right. That is 000010.1 $0.00010\,1 \times 10^5 = 10.1$

3. Area = square feet ; length = 3.812×10^2 feet
    Area = length × width

    Thus width will be $\dfrac{5.352048 \times 10^4}{3.812 \times 10^2} = 1.404 \times 10^{4-2} = 1.404 \times 10^2$ feet

Mini-Assessment

1 The world is estimated to have 7,169,000,000 people. What would this be in scientific notation?

A. 7.169×10^{-9} B. 0.7169×10^{-10} C. 0.7169×10^{10} D. 7.169×10^{9} E. 7.0×10^{9}

2 Which of the following numbers is rational?

A. e^2 B. $\dfrac{2\pi^2}{\sqrt{2}}$ C. $\left(\dfrac{e^3}{e^3\sqrt{2}+e^3\sqrt{2}}\right)^2$ D. $\dfrac{\phi^2}{\sqrt{5}}$ E. $\phi + e$

3 The mass of one atom of hydrogen gas is 1.007825 amu (atomic mass unit). What would be the mass of atoms?

A. 4.43443×10^{5} B. 4.43443×10^{6} C. 4.43443×10^{-5} D. 4.43443×10^{-6} E 4.43443×10^{4}

4 The thickness of one book is 2.0×10^{-1} feet. If the book 8.42×10^{2} papers, find the thickness of one paper.

5 The thickness of hairs is approximately 8.42×10^{2} millimeter. If 1 millimeter = 0.03937 inches, find the thickness of hair in inches.

6 John had $\$8.4 \times 10^{4}$ in her bank. He spent 10^{-2} of the amount on funding a construction project and 2.0×10^{-2} of the amount on contributing to begin an cone processing company. How much does he remains with?

7 A water reservoir has 3.14×10^{6} cubic feet of water. It looses 2.0×10^{-2} % cubic feet of water through evaporation and absorption in a day. What is the approximate volume of water in the reservoir at the end of the day given that the habitats uses 4.14×10^{3} cubic feet only a day.

Mini-Assessment Answers

1 D.

To get the value of a, we put the decimal point between 7 and 1, $a = 7.169$
The initial position of the decimal point is after the last zero; by putting the decimal between 7 and 1: it will have moved 9 steps to the left, thus $n = 9$

$7,169,000,000 = 7.169 \times 10^9$

2 C

is an irrational number , due to its definition, its square will also be an irrational number

$e \times e = e^2$ is irrational

$2\pi^2$ is irrational

$\dfrac{2\pi^2}{\sqrt{2}}$ because the square of pi is irrational

is irrational because the product of an irrational and a rational number is an irrational number
is an irrational number because the division of two irrational numbers that are not equal is an

irrational number $\left(\dfrac{e^3}{e^3\sqrt{2}+e^3\sqrt{2}}\right)^2 = \left(\dfrac{e^3}{2e^3\sqrt{2}}\right)^2 = \left(\dfrac{1}{2\sqrt{2}}\right)^2 = \dfrac{1}{(2\sqrt{2})^2} = \dfrac{1}{2^2(\sqrt{2})^2} = \dfrac{1}{4\sqrt{2}\times\sqrt{2}} = \dfrac{1}{4\times 2} = \dfrac{1}{8}$

This is a rational number
We do not have to test the next option, thus the answer is C

3 A

One atom is equal to is 1.007825 amu
atoms will be equal to $4.4\times10^5 \times 1.007825 = 4.43443\times10^5 \, amu$

4 thickness of the one book = 2.0×10^{-1} feet

the number of papers = 8.42×10^2 papers

One paper will have a thickness of $\dfrac{2.0\times10^{-1}}{8.42\times10^2} = \dfrac{1}{4.21}\times10^{-1-2} = 0.2375\times10^{-3}$ feet

Changing to standard form, we have $0.2375\times10^{-3} = 2.375\times10^{-4}$ feet

5 Thickness = 8.0×10^{-2} millimeter

1 millimeter = 0.03937 inches = 3.937×10^{-2} inches

8.0×10^{-2} millimeter = 3.937×10^{-2} = $8.0 \times 10^{-2} \times 3.937 \times 10^{-2}$ = 31.496×10^{-4}

$3.1496 \times 10^{1} \times 10^{-4}$ We write the number in scientific notation

$= 3.1496 \times 10^{-3}$ inches

6 Total amount in the bank = $\$8.4 \times 10^{4} = \$84,000$

Amount spent on construction project = $10^{-2} \times \$8.4 \times 10^{4} = \$8.4 \times 10^{4-2}$
Contribution to the company = $2.0 \times 10^{-2} \times 8.4 \times 10^{4} = 2.0 \times 10^{-2} \times 8.4 \times 10^{4} = 2.0 \times 8.4 \times 10^{4} \times 10^{-2}$
We write the number in scientific notation $= 16.8 \times 10^{4-2}$
The difference is $\$84,000 - \$840 - \$1680 = \$81,480$
In scientific notation, we have $\$8.148 \times 10^{4}$

7 Water in the reservoir = 3.14×10^{6} cubic feet = 3,140,000 cubic feet

$$2.0 \times 10^{-2}\% = \frac{2.0 \times 10^{-2}}{100} = \frac{2.0 \times 10^{-2}}{10^{2}} = 2.0 \times 10^{-2-2} = 2.0 \times 10^{-4}$$

Lose on evaporation and absorption = $2.0 \times 10^{-4} \times 3.14 \times 10^{6} = 2.0 \times 3.14 \times 10^{6-4} = 6.28 \times 10^{2} = 628$ cubic feet
Use by the habitat = 4.14×10^{3} = 4140 cubic feet
The remaining volume of water is $3140000 - 628 - 4140 = \$3,135,232$
Writing in scientific notation, we have $\$3.135232 \times 10^{6}$

Lesson Reflection

- In this lesson, we have learned about irrational numbers where we discussed that it is a number that cannot be expressed as h/k where h and k are integers and k cannot be zero. Examples pi =π. We went ahead to introduce scientific notation , a representation that is widely used in representing numbers is a more compact form. Finally, we have looked at a away that we can work with the numbers written in scientific notation. These implies the rules of exponents that allows as multiply, divide and carry out other operations on numbers having exponents.

- We have also discussed a few instances where the scientific notation, exponents and irrational numbers are applied in the real life situations.

www.ingramcontent.com/pod-product-compliance
Lightning Source LLC
Chambersburg PA
CBHW081452070426
42452CB00042B/2685